Five Years Old
and I Gotta
Know

Five Years Old and I Gotta Know

*Most stories start somewhere at sometime
The present to the future choices make a difference
Check It Out*

ReadersMagnet, LLC

GREGORY BOOTH

Five Years Old and I Gotta Know
Copyright © 2019 by Gregory Booth

Published in the United States of America
ISBN Paperback: 978-1-949981-40-7
ISBN eBook: 978-1-949981-41-4

All rights reserved. No part of this publication may be reproduced, stored in a retrieval system or transmitted in any way by any means, electronic, mechanical, photocopy, recording or otherwise without the prior permission of the author except as provided by USA copyright law.

Scriptures marked KJV are taken from *King James Version* (KJV): *King James Version*, public domain.

The opinions expressed by the author are not necessarily those of ReadersMagnet, LLC.

ReadersMagnet, LLC
10620 Treena Street, Suite 230 | San Diego, California, 92131 USA
1.619. 354. 2643 | www.readersmagnet.com

Book design copyright © 2019 by ReadersMagnet, LLC. All rights reserved.
Cover design by Ericka Walker
Interior design by Shemaryl Evans

Contents

Preface: A Person's Salvation and a Church's Restoration 7
Chapter One: My Name 9
Chapter Two: My Formation 13
Chapter Three: Life Begins 20
Chapter Four: Return Home 24
Chapter Five: I Am Dead 30
Chapter Six: Forgiven 35
Chapter Seven: Choosing Help 39
Chapter Eight: Has Happened to Others Too 46
Chapter Nine: Things in Life 51
Chapter Ten: Overwhelmed 58
Chapter Eleven: Blessings to Be Had 62
Afterword 65
Vocabulary Notes 72

Preface

A Person's Salvation and a Church's Restoration

At the present time, there are those who do not know Jesus as Savior or Lord. They are lost.

Not only are there individuals who do not know God, but there are churches that have become less than lukewarm.

Most of my life I've had people tell me this: if you can't say anything good, don't say anything at all. The churches have adopted this as a primary directive and use it to omit accountability.

Today the church is weak and to some extent has lost its way. The doctrines of men and the ease of seduction by Satan are diminishing God's importance to the church.

The acts occurring in our nation are a testimony to the compromising of our morals and faith in God. The churches should hold their members accountable for their actions instead of looking the other way.

When people are accountable to the leading of God's Word then they will carry this into everyday life. Men of

God need to stand on the principles set in God's Word, without compromising. Perhaps they don't have time with all that needs to be done; discipline helps set priorities.

The expectation for failure is due to the lack of preparation. This comes from either the lack or offering of the principles to the members of the church or the lack of motivation on behalf of the individuals to receive those principles.

The offerings of Satan are very appealing and with little resistance from the recipient of the invitation. How much more is the pressure on those who have no set of moral studies?

Chapter One

My Name

My name is Work In Progress. I was born in the city of Pendleton, Oregon, in June of 1948. Yes, my life started nine months earlier; however it wasn't until much later than the time it started that I could remember details. All I can recall from before I was five years old is that I had curiosity within me, and I was an investigator of all I could see and know around me.

My story really begins in May of my fourth year. I was an investigator whose little legs carried me every direction that my mom would let me go, and often where she didn't.

This first day of my story began just off the back steps on the sidewalk behind the house I grew up in. Oh! Yes, I guess I had better mention this aspect of my life at the time: I liked the other kids in the neighborhood well enough and would play with them, but only for short periods of time. I needed to find out how things worked, and that is where I spent most of my time. That was what I sought out for fun.

Now back to the sidewalk, at the back of the house. Today was unusual because I was looking to play; well, at least for a while. But as I stood there listening, I couldn't hear any other kids playing in my neighborhood. What a strange thing! There was always noise from my generation because of the normal screams and yelling the kids my age generated every day of the week. My next-older brother was five and a half years my senior and you could always tell which part of the neighborhood he was in. But today was quiet, with no sounds to be heard anywhere.

The only noise I could hear was coming from my mother, who was cleaning the flowerbed next to the little cottage behind our house. I wanted to play so badly that day I asked my mom if she would play with me. But her answer was she needed to get her flowers planted. So I guess I was out of luck. I stood there for some time, remembering how my mother would tell me I should always behave because God was watching and he would tell her. Then I would be in trouble.

Knowing God heard things and that he would tell my mom, I thought if He talked to her then He could talk to me also. So I looked up at the sky between two trees in the backyard sort of up and to my right, and said, "God, can you come and play with me as no one seems to be around?"

To my surprise, I got an answer. The answer was almost like my mother's answer in that God said, "I can't come right now. It isn't time. I still need to get some things done." So I asked if he had time to talk for a while; He said yes.

Well, I asked many things, I'm sure. Being in God's presence was very enjoyable. After a while, my mother asked, "Who are you talking to?" So I told her and she didn't say anything, just kept working. My conversation with God got interrupted after a while. It seems some of the neighborhood kids were playing in the hedge across the street at my aunt's house.

Well, they interrupted my talk with God by asking me to come over and see what they were doing. I said to them I was talking to God, that I would come later.

As I continued to talk to God, God told me not to go over there. I knew right away something must be wrong. I said to God, "If there is something wrong, maybe I should go and put a stop to it before things get out of hand."

"I wouldn't go if I were you," God replied.

So I just stayed and talked with God some more. All the while, the kids kept calling me. Finally I said to God, "If you go with me, I won't have to worry because you can stop anything that is wrong because you are God."

Well, God said to me, "If you go over there, I can't be with you any longer." At that point, God quit speaking to me.

I decided to answer the call of the other children. I was prepared for conflict. As I strutted across the street I was confident God would not let me down. I knew inside that he cared for me, and that he didn't want those kids in trouble either. After all I was four years and elven months old; and it made perfect sense to me.

I reached the fence and climbed over where there was a small space between the hedge bushes. Just on the other side, I found my friends. Immediately, I could see why God didn't want me to go over there. I guess as they were playing earlier, someone brought up the differences in how people use the toilet. Well, to prove who was right, my peers had exposed themselves and were comparing the differences in plumbing fixtures. As I came over the fence and saw what was happening, I lit into them right away. I told them God knew that they were up to no good and had better stop.

I did this with all the swagger and toughness I could muster. All three were willing to fight, but somehow talk was in order.

They began to explain what they were doing and why. They said that no one had to know they did it, that if I wanted to fight, it would be three against one. But I shouldn't be worried, because they just wanted to know the differences in how to use the toilet.

Remember me saying how I was an investigator and wanted to know how things worked?

Well, the wisdom of my peers overcame my vigilance, and curiosity took control. After all, one of them was almost six years old and had much greater wisdom than the rest of us had.

I put up my vigilance in the fight for right, which gave way to mutual curiosity in twenty seconds or so. Now I am also a follower of this scientific research. What have you done lately?

What was the outcome for your efforts? Today is no different from any other period in history. The technology of the day may be different, but man is still of the same design as any other period of history.

Man is still involved in thinking his own ways are more profitable than the way which God set things into motion. In chapter 2 of Genesis, we will look at some of the things God set into motion.

Chapter Two

My Formation

In Genesis 2:4–5, we see the first mention of God's design of man's purpose and function before the ground could be blessed with rain coming down from heaven. There had to be a man who could be a follower of instructions on how to till the ground. He had to be willing to engage in the directions laid out for him to follow.

As I read these two verses, I find a divine plan which preceded the earth's building project by God's design. I also see that the love of God is so deep that I'm not at this point able to put into it the words necessary to bring even a small portion of it to light.

Please let me attempt to show what these two verses mean to me. Have you ever risen early in the morning and gone outside to see the sun rising at the break of day?

Here is the bathing of new life on the intricate texture of fine artwork, with a superbly designed relationship to the workings of God. Each created form of life waits to meet God's breath upon them for each new day. The trees' needles or leaves begin to sway as the sun heats the atmosphere and air currents begin to move the foliage and its branches. Even the weeds that have little flowers open to greet the great coming dawn.

The awakening brings a rejoicing in being present to witness and testify to the loving grace of God.

Now think on this: all the plants and their design fit harmoniously with expectation in relationship to functioning with each other in order of design to bring support and comfort and yes, even to give direction. Their very being is a testimony to love expressed as life is continually repeated through their fruitfulness.

In verse 5 of Genesis 2, God tells us plainly that all these plants were fashioned before they were ever placed on the earth. Before there could be rain, it took a man to till the ground and to have oversight on the government of nature, ruling over proliferation by advantage and not design purpose. Man, being created in the image of God and under the direction of God's instruction, would bless all forms of life managed by God's instruction.

Now, in chapter 2, verse 8, this passage plainly states who planted the garden. And whose garden was it? Who do you think it belonged to? I think all things made by someone, which are made out of their own resources, belong to them and should be held in governance of the design of the one who made it.

The garden of God was completely furnished and made ready for occupancy by God. Also, the man, God's administrator, together with all of the other fashioning of God, which Scripture tells us was formed by God are the property of God

The instruction of God was sufficient to Adam (the one formed by God). To know what was required to perform the administrational duties of being an administrator.

First we see God's instruction as what to do in verse 15 (King James Version). And God took the man and put him into the garden of Eden to dress it and keep it.

Second thing God did was command the man in verses 16–17 (KJV). "And the Lord God commanded the man, saying, Of every tree of the garden thou mayest freely eat: But of the tree of the knowledge of good and evil, thou shalt not eat of it: for in the day thou eatest thereof thou shalt surely die."

Now this parallels the instruction God gave me on that sidewalk at four to five years of age. Let's look at some of the similarities.

When speaking with God and the other kids were calling me, I told them I would come over later. God spoke to me from the love which motivates Him in all things and said, "Do not go over there." When I reasoned with God, He said, "I would not go over there if I was you." When I felt bound to go, God said to me, "If you go over there, I cannot be with you anymore."

What did I do? I heard three instructions from the creator God saying not to go. Instead, I listened to the plea of my peers. I was out of character as to the normal desires of my nature as I sought to play that day. I thought because God spoke to me that I had influence with God and He would capitulate and come to my rescue if I got into trouble. After all, my mom would tell me God loved me. So even if I wasn't doing what He said, love would override direction. And I could get my own way!

What I see looking back from the present to that time is that I was accountable for what I knew and was instructed to do. And I think of how easily my good intentions could be disarmed and how quickly reason could seduce a person into participation. By justifying the terms of the situation, this is called being seduced, or, in other terms, eating from the tree of knowledge of good and evil.

So there I was, no longer in the garden with God, having speaking privileges with God.

Before I go on with my testimony, I would like to show an illustration I got from the Lord. Here are the following points that I hope will bring some light into how things work:

1. The vertical line represents the life God has given us.

2. It represents the access point we have with God.

3. The upper triangle goes to infinity. And blessing and protection of God are showered on us. Like the rain in the garden of Eden.

4. The lower triangle represents God's protection.

5. It represents me. I am well protected in this view.

6. It represents the tree of the knowledge of good and evil, the only other source able to reach our access point. This is the only access allowed in the garden of Eden, which is the protected part of God's dwelling.

7. This base line represents God's protection as long as we are surrounded by light and truth and filled with the abundance of God's presence.

See the illustrations below.

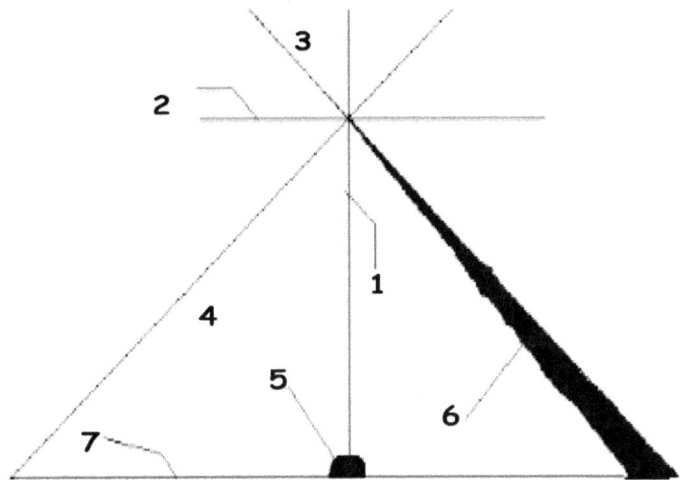

Before God's protection is removed.

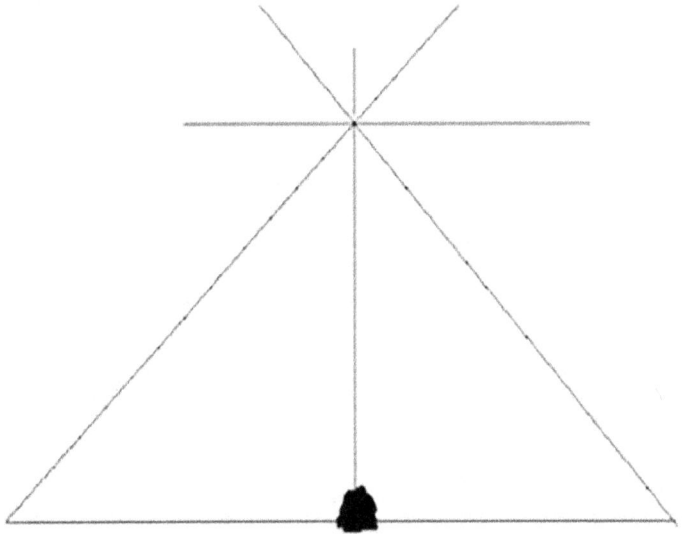

After God's protection is removed, and God's protective influences begin to be denied by the fallen person. They are less able to defend against the attacks and influences of others on their life.

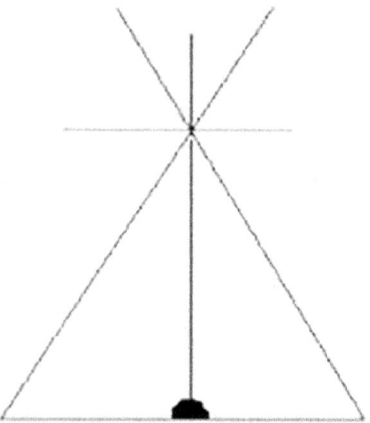

The more influence of others in our lives. There is less ability to stand on our own power.

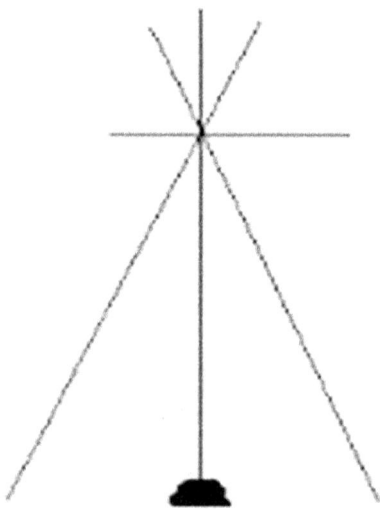

When both God's blessing and access have been fully denied by a person, there is no light for him or her to draw on through his or her own ability.

For God to change our lives, He must come through the access point of our lives. At this point, access by us is not possible. But God has another way. John 3:16: "For God so loved the world, that he gave his only begotten Son, that whosoever believeth in him should not perish, but have everlasting life."

Please forgive my drawings, they are crude but I hope they relate the understanding.

Chapter Three

LIFE BEGINS

Here a life, which God did not want for me to have, *begins.* The encounter which I had, at the moment I began to view the very thing that God did not want me to be involved in, took charge of my life. I was successfully seduced by Satan's plan to defile everyone and everything.

Genesis 2:16–17 "and the Lord God commanded the man, saying, Of every tree of the garden thou mayest freely eat: but of the tree of the knowledge of good and evil, thou shalt not eat of it; for in the day that thou eatest thereof thou shalt surely die."

The command that God gave to Adam and Eve was the same command God gave me when He said, "Do not go over there." Now look at what the sinful nature of Adam and Eve, imparted to all their decedents, brought to pass.

The second thing God said to me was, "I would not go over there if I was you." This was after I reasoned with God. This was my thoughts, from my mind, and it did not change God's instruction. Is this not what Satan did to Eve—reason with her—and she changed her mind?

Here we see the voice of Satan, who gained entrance to all human life through the original sin, which happened in the Garden of Eden with Eve and Adam, participating in eating the forbidden fruit.

The garden contained only those things which God had created. John 1:3 "says; all things were made by him; and without Him was not anything made that was made."

Now! Was the separation of God and man? Genesis 3:22–24 says, "And the Lord God said, behold, the man is become as one of us, to know good and evil: and now, lest he put forth his hand, and take also of the tree of life, and eat, and live forever: Therefore the Lord God sent him forth from the Garden of Eden, to till the ground from whence he was taken. So they drove out the man; and placed at the east of the Garden of Eden Cherubim's, and a flaming sword which turned away, to keep the way of the tree of life."

Here is like what happened to me, except there was no need to remove me from the garden as I was never in it. Here is where the innocence of my youth was not able to keep me, and God had departed from me, knowing the outcome of my thoughts. As we are born in sin, it isn't far we have to go to be in over our heads.

The days at first were not much different from before. As time went on, it was easier to investigate the unknown, of what had taken place as I crossed that fence. The pull to know more about what these pluming instruments were for began to take hold of thoughts, and it was not long before we discovered another use of male and female plumbing parts and how they go together.

Remember the illustration I showed earlier? Well, it was taking effect. As the sinful nature began to grow the precepts of judgment; our conscience weakened. The more the sinful nature grew, the weaker we became, until the struggle to do right was very hard.

Here is where in my life the battle began. I still knew better but came to the place where I did not have power to push out the wrong thoughts coming into my mind. The stronger they became, the more my mind hurt; it hurt so bad that I wanted to die.

At this point, I gave up everything in my private time to think about these unholy, unrighteous, killing thoughts. I began to seek out different ways to gratify my impulses. I became the vilest person I knew.

Though I would ask God to help me, I never was able to stop what I was doing. However; I believe God prevented me from ever hurting anyone. All the way through school, I keep ahold of my actions, as to the depth of my thoughts, which almost cost me my mind.

After high school, I went to work for the Kerns Company in Pilot Rock, Oregon. This provided some control in my life. But I didn't have victory, just a tool that helped me control what was in my mind.

I received an invitation to join Uncle Sam's military service. So I joined the navy, and for three years and eight months I had both the freedom and the means to let all my inhibitions go. I let evil thoughts have their way. I was the worst for having done it, engaging in much of what I had tried not to do before getting out of high school.

When sitting in a nightclub in New Jersey, the voice of the Lord spoke to my mind. It told me to go home because I was in trouble. This was the same voice that I talked with when I was five years old. The very next day, I made arrangements to fly home.

Up to this point, I have left out the verbal pictures of what I'd done. Because most know, or have their own mental pictures, of what a sinful man does.

Chapter Four

RETURN HOME

I arrived back home after a few hours of flying. It was the last week of January, 1971.

Here I started to take the measure of myself; and it was not a pretty picture. I began again to seek God for help. He heard, and little by little I began to see how one can overcome the impossible.

During this time, I had migraine headaches so bad and nothing would stop them or even make them easier.

One day, a Sunday, my head hurt so bad that I had to do something to lessen the pain. So I took hold of the door casing and relaxed as much as possible, and then jerked my arms quickly so I wouldn't prepare for what was coming: the impact of my head when it hit the doorjamb.

Needless to say, my mom didn't raise all her boys to have smarts, as I had to find out in my own way.

The hit on *the old cranium* brought another solution. Here's how it went: I said, "God, just kill me?" He answered me back, "Why don't you call on the Lord?" I was thinking this was a trick of Satan because, even though I believed it was God who had sent me home, I still remembered what God had said to me when I was five years old: "I cannot be with you anymore."

So I thought on this for a while and decided this must have been God who spoke to me. I then said to God if he would heal me of these headaches, I would serve him for the rest of my life. That was a Sunday morning near noontime. About a half hour later, I decided to go out and get the family Bible and take it to the kitchen to find out what to do next.

When I opened the Bible up, it started the longest day of my life; when I began looking through it to see if there was a starting place, I landed on the book of Acts as I figured I could relate to it.

Well, this is definitely the hardest thing I have ever done in my life. Acts chapter 1, verse 1. I started around 12:30 p.m. and finished after 5:00 p.m. Oh yes, this was in March, 1971.

I know you are probably asking yourself, "Has this guy lost his marbles or something? Four hours to read one verse of Scripture?" Hey, as long as you don't laugh, I'm okay with it! Yes, it did take that long.

Here's the story about this event: when deciding to read Acts 1:1, I didn't know you had to chase the words down before you could read them. Okay! You think this guy is short a couple of cards of having a full deck or something like that. I see your point! But it happened just that way; *whenever I* looked at the first word, it shot off across the page and hid among the other words. I at first didn't know how I was going to find the word. Then I saw a word that was misaligned with the other words on the page.

I then fixed my eyes on it and was able to drag it back into place. As long as I didn't take my eyes off of it, it stayed until I read the word. Then it never moved again. But the next word did, and so it was with all the words I read.

Before I put the Bible away, I thought I would see if this was the case throughout the Bible. I checked many books and found it to be so, and by unrelenting perseverance I found *only* one book of the Bible I could read: the book of Job. I could read it like a comic book or any other book I chose to read.

Job I read over and over, and I still enjoy reading it today; it prepared me for the long haul. Before I was able to read any of the other books, I had to do word searches. When doing this, I was able to read the words that gave the meaning of the word I was looking up and I could read them. After many months, I was able to read the entire Bible in any way I sought.

The Bible reading was of great comfort during this time. However there was something going on at the same time that took a heavy toll on my life. From the first night I spent after asking Jesus into my life (I was twenty-two years old) until I was in the summer of my forty-eighth year, I was raped by a demonic spirit.

I would go to bed each night and read my Bible from fifteen minutes to two hours. I prayed for all my family and friends. I prayed for our nation and the church which I attended. I would go to sleep saying "Jesus, Jesus, Jesus" over and over; still sometime in the middle of the night it would happen.

Can you imagine this happening to someone over and over, when you have asked your Lord and Savior to deliver you from this night after night? It would seem to say I was not born again, would it not?

I have thought on this from time to time, and what is the difference now compared with when it was happening? Someone will surely say I was not truly born again, that I was never born again or believed.

All I know is the Bible says that the word is as close as your mouth; ask and you will receive. Romans 10:8 and 9 "But what saith it? The word is nigh thee, *even* in thy mouth, and in thy heart: that is, the word of faith, which we preach; that if thou shalt confess with thy mouth the Lord Jesus, and shalt believe in thy heart that God hath raised him from the dead, thou shalt be saved."

During the time I've walked with the Lord, even that time, many people may think I never knew Him. Satan tried to kill me many times.

When I returned home after the service from the Navy, I was weak and couldn't expend too much energy without becoming very sick. The VA doctors tried to tell me it was because I was depressed. I am not a doctor, but to me depression was when the will was weak and there was not drive. I cannot think of such a time in my life. I have always been seeking to do or help in anyway available. I am someone not willing to be held out of what is going on and will not stand for it to be that way in my life.

No matter what is going on, it goes on. I gradually gained strength. I seemed to overcome that time in my life.

In 1982–1985, I again underwent much pain. There was so much that I cannot describe it; I can only say that each morning when I awoke from sleep would be pleasant, and all would be right with the world. This was at the moment I opened my eyes. When I moved my eyes to look around, the pain would shoot through me like a strike of lightning or a shot of electricity.

Two and one half years this happened every morning. Only three muscle groups worked without pain: my heart, the muscles that worked my lungs, and my eyelids.

The pain was too great to get out of bed, but I found a way to get out of bed. I would lie there and think of anything that would make me mad! And I would think on it until a shot of adrenalin hit me. At that instant, I would jump out of bed and that would give a bigger shot of adrenalin to enable me to dress.

From that point on I would not stop moving. I cut and sold firewood in those days. The harder I worked, the less pain I had. So by the time evening came, it was tolerable and I could rest at night.

I believe the Lord guided me in getting rid of the pain. About six months before the pain subsided, I was praying and asking God to do anything that would relieve me of this pain. The next day I started receiving five pieces of natural-healing mail and this mail came every day. About three to five pieces of mail came daily until about three months before the pain started to let up. I got mail on how to cook dark-green vegetables at a low heat to preserve the enzymes. I ate this three times a day for the last three months.

During this time, 85 percent or more of the pain left my body. After that I ate eggs and fresh green vegetables, drank lots of water, and began to incorporate meats and grains. I was pain free after about a year.

Was I saved? If believing after asking is a requirement, then yes I was. Why these things worked in my life I can only guess at this time.

It would seem to me that one who endures great tribulation may be more prepared to face the hopelessness of whatever may come upon himself or other people he cares about in the future.

I do pray to be released from tests and trials which the future may bring. But I will not turn away from God if this is not the case.

Jesus said we would suffer as He suffered and not have a good day every moment. What Jesus did was suffer the attacks of sin all men experience. I hope to stay with God while suffering whatever attacks come on my life.

Chapter Five

I Am Dead

Cancer was the next major disease to attack my life. I was at that point where for a number of years my strength had become less and less. Sickness of all kinds would find their way into my life. This made life unbearable for me.

The years after that were more consistent. My health grew weaker by degree and there wasn't much of an up-and-down kind of thing going on in my life. I took jobs working as a contractor doing remodeling jobs. I worked hard and did not fool around. My day was devoted to doing a full day's work for my money. My customers got the full contract agreement; both of us were thankful when the job was done. Myself a little weaker, but the work performed met the customers' satisfaction. As did all my jobs.

In March, 1989, I took a job painting the inside of a friend's house. On the day I arrived to start the work, I noticed that my friend Ed had a very sad look about him. Doris, Ed's wife, said that he had just had a cancer tumor taken out of his prostate. There were some complications. The doctor had left a tool inside and had to go back in and take it out. The doctor said that he wanted Ed to take chemotherapy. This was the last thing that Ed wanted to do. Ed had already watched two daughters die from taking chemotherapy. Now doctors wanted *him* to take it! No way.

Ed at some point had contacted a naturopathic doctor. This doctor told him he could probably put the cancer into remission, and without toxic chemotherapy. Ed's large family didn't want him to see the naturopathic doctor. They wanted to have the regular medical doctor treat him.

As I spoke with Ed, he told me of his options. Then he said, "What you would do if you were me?"

I told him that for as long as I have known him that he'd been telling me of the natural things one can do to be healthy. So I told him to try the naturopathic doctor. Ed decided to do so. Then he suggested that I go with him and get myself checked out.

There was a nurse from a cancer research hospital in California who had been coming once a year for the last few years. She came to observe what the doctor was doing. The doctor spoke with Ed about half an hour then took blood and saliva and was in the back office for at least forty-five minutes doing tests. When he came out, he explained what Ed needed to do and how to do it. Then Ed spoke to him and said his friend needed some looking at also. Ed asked, "Have you time to check him out?" The doctor did, so I gave some blood and saliva for him to test.

During the time the doctor was in the back office, the nurse spoke of her husband and how this doctor was able to get her husband over the effects of the cancer. He had been given one to three months to live by the doctors at the cancer research hospital in California. And now, after being treated by this naturopath, was in total remission. He was back working at his job as a building contractor.

During our visit, while the doctor was doing my tests, the nurse mentioned that he was taking longer than he had ever taken before. That in fact it had been more than twice as long.

The doctor came back into the room after finishing the tests. He didn't say anything for some time. He just looked at the nurse. And then he looked at me with his hands on his hips. Finally he spoke: "I do not know how to say this but to just tell you. You are dead." Then he said, "I know you aren't dead at this moment, but there is nothing I can do for you. The tests indicate that you have over three times the cancer of anyone I have ever checked. And most of my patients have one to three months to live, when they come to me. I have done your tests twice because I thought surely I'd made a mistake. But in the end, the test results were the same."

As the doctor went on speaking, he told me that if he treated me and I died, the word would always get out. Others whom he could help would not come to see him, as naturopathic doctors are held to different standards than other doctors. In the medical world the news media would make a big stink out of it.

Immediately upon hearing this, the nurse said, "You treat him just as you treated my husband." The doctor replied, "Your husband didn't come close to having this much cancer in his body."

There are no known cases of anyone surviving this kind of onset. Everyone in that room heard the conversation at that moment. I spoke to the doctor and said, "I know something you do not know, that in 1979 the Lord spoke to me audibly or loudly in my mind and told me I would never die of cancer. If you treat me, no one in my life would speak about you treating me if I should die." He said, "It isn't that I won't treat you, it's that if I do and you die, it always seems that word gets out and others whom I can help would maybe not come. However I will if you want me to."

The doctor treated me. And in the same time period as all the rest of his patients, I was free of any living cancer cells. However my blood was littered with dead cells and my body was having a hard time cleaning them out. My body was finally able to remove all the dead cells after a period of time.

Note: This *doctor* prayed for all his patients each day by name and need. Starting at around 3:30 p.m., the doctor prayed until he had finished praying for all.

The doctor told me it took on average around one to three years for a patient to regain the harmony of his body organs. He said it may take me three years to even twelve years. Also I maybe would never be able to have harmony in my organs again. For eleven to twelve years my food would not digest completely and my bowels had trouble eliminating the waste without help. Praise the Lord I have overcome!

Since I've overcome the cancer, I have had other attacks on my body, such as acid-reflex disease, pneumonia, airborne allergies, arthritis pain, diverticulitis, melanosis, and other ailments. Oh, yeah! I also had a self-diagnosed disease (dummy's disease), which is defined as working more hours than your body can handle. This has caused me to once more have trouble with my bowels, and I still have arthritis pain. Does the merry-go-round ever stop?

No matter! This is still the most blessed life I could hope for. For you see, the Lord died for me. I am saved! Once you find this solution to life, it is all downhill no matter how bad things get. I'm not preaching right now—maybe later on in the book.

Chapter Six

FORGIVEN

Do you know what it means to be forgiven? Let me give it a try: it means that whatever you did in your life that brought some kind of pain or discomfort, through and act or word to others, is no longer held against you by the ones who received the offense.

It is not ignoring the matter until no one remembers it any longer. It is not something you can do for yourself unless it pertains to your assessment of yourself. Sometimes we can be pretty hard on ourselves. It is, however, acts of grace, the unmerited response of one of the victims of our actions or words, which says, "I will not hold you responsible for what has taken place through your actions or words."

Forgiveness is the courage of the oppressed to make away for the oppressor to receive a choice he would not otherwise have had. This brings opportunity for reconciliation. Now in my life I didn't take God's words to me to be of importance and went ahead and did what I thought was right in my own understanding. Remember at the first of this book when I was five years old? How I didn't listen to God's words and did my own thing? The question is not whether I did myself physical harm right then and there. The future, however, would bring reality to what I did.

What I did was to ignore the advice of someone who had the knowledge of the outcome of the actions I would take. The result of this proved to be more than my little mind wanted to know. It has been the same for others since time began on this planet.

All the years I've suffered in the way I did, through the illnesses, may not have occurred if I had just listened to what God had spoken to me. I will never know in this life if I would have had a continual speaking relationship with God in which I could ask for His advice and He would give it any time I needed it.

The whole story of my life is within my soul's experience. Should I tell all of it in detail or just caution others to be alert to the things around them? I think most have had similar experiences. But all may not have had the realization of what took place. I'm no great expert on the subject but can tell you there is something more than just being alive.

When I disobeyed God, I put into action my own outlook on how things were going to be for my life. That was to do as I deemed right. I would be the judge of what I thought was right. Now we all know there are more than just ourselves who live on this planet and we have to interact with one another on a daily basis. So if they live according to the same philosophy as I do, we're not going to get along very well, are we?

Do you know the scientific law about how two things are not able to occupy the same space at the same time? If they do, it means they had to combine their elements somehow and become something different from what they were at the start. A whole lot of compromise! Well, I like being me probably as much as you like being you, so we know that won't likely happen.

Here is where the words God spoke to me came into play. God set up this world so that it could work without too much difficulty. What would you expect from God anyway? God is the high point in everything; nothing exists without God. Right! Right! Okay, let's see how I went wrong in the beginning.

I did know who I was speaking to. I knew without a doubt. I regarded God as some nice guy that wanted to give me some advice, not as God who has the only correct and direct path for the advice He gives.

This is a God who loves me so much that to give me advice which is not correct would not even be thinkable on His part. What this means is to ignore God and make yourself the discerner of all your knowledge based on what your experiences have taught you. Now you are at the age of accountability. Your actions from this time forward will determine the outcome of your life. You have moved into the DIY mode. Do you have the knowledge base and experience to manage the rest of your life alone?

At five years old, you would think I could leap tall buildings, be more powerful than a locomotive, and move certainly faster than a speeding bullet. Is this where Superman came from, the thoughts of a five-year-old? Well, as I shared in chapter 1, I thought I could go over there and straighten out anything that was wrong. And this was the beginning of sorrows for me.

The sorrows lasted until I was graced by God to receive word from God's mouth, inviting me to call on Jesus for salvation. This brought forgiveness and a new direction of learning. I now have a willingness to trust the leading of the Holy Spirit in my life.

I have not regretted calling on the Lord's invitation to make him Lord of my life. The journey has been full. The hardships of the past have given way to the trials of life, learning to discern between the leading of God's Word and being lured by Satan to mock God.

Through the guidance of the Holy Spirit, I'm learning to follow sound instruction. What chance does a five-year-old have of overcoming the whiles of Satan in this world today? Anyone think we are alone to maneuver the days of our lives without confrontation? Think again!

The time is stuffed with options and ideas that come from so many sources that making one day fruitful is a task in itself. Remember the tree bears fruit of its own kind. There are many who want to poison the fruit of righteousness and have their own fruit to be the way of the future.

The hardships in the past that I endured were the result of leaning on my own understanding without help from God. God is just but also is right in all things. And though He gives us many chances to know Him, He does not have to give any chance once He's judged us to be disobedient. God's mercy endures. If we seek Him, he will see our approach. If we call on Him, He will forgive.

In the trials of life are the ways men meet each day. It is in the decisions each one makes that determines how the day will play out in the end. There is a gauntlet of many views and paths that present themselves. Which require the gravest consideration on our part? Even one wrong choice can kill all that remains of a person's life. However no one who falls in Christ will be without hope of resurrection. For all others, the way is lost.

Chapter Seven

CHOOSING HELP

What does *repentance* or *to repent* mean? The meaning I've drawn from research incorporates the following: Knowing there are moral standards which are the basis for right and wrong. All have been in the contact of rules and standards of human behavior. We see virtue as being capable of following those standards that are reflective of those things which arise in the mind and bring into alignment the understanding of our imagination.

When the standards of moral human behavior are weakened by other influences, then we are no longer virtuous and are unable to keep the standards of behavior which govern our actions by the exercise of our willingness to acknowledge those very standards.

Here is one aspect of not following those standards: as sorrows which bring unrest into our lives. Through a course of study in the Bible, we are able to see this being acted out. And we see where the moral standards and rules come from. They come from the God who created all things.

When there is a denial of these standards, and rules, which come from God; this will fashion separation from the compunction to observe moral behavior. This behavior was restored for those who would receive the gospel of Jesus Christ. This was accomplished by the Holy Spirit in revealing to the understanding of the mind of man for the purpose of invitation to receive. There is great help for anyone who seeks release from the sins of the past. Whosoever calls on the Lord Jesus Christ will be saved, according to the Scripture found in John 3:16.

There is repentance which is called for. John the Baptist has shown us this aspect of salvation: Jesus Christ, who is our Savior, was obedient to receive baptism from John the Baptist.

Repentance is the reconsideration of that compunction and acting upon it to receive salvation. This is only possible through the impartation of the Holy Spirit in the lives of the potential recipient. All will have the opportunity to receive the restoration of that compunction.

So the sorrows that God allows in a person's life will come to the light of their purpose when held up to the commandments of God's law. When one acknowledges a comparison between God's laws, which is the regent for God, to the sorrows of those which know not God, will promote a moral feeling of compunction. This is to think differently or afterward of knowing such sorrows. You are at this point able to choose the offer of salvation that has been presented to you.

Is this not a result of the work of the Holy Spirit working to drawing us to the saving Grace of our Lord, Jesus?

There have been many teachings on this which have shed light on how we repent and what takes place. I hope that I have been able to bring a little light to this subject.

I know this: that Satan does not know the word *quit*. He will hit you from every direction and take pleasure in it. Even though he will never overcome God, he wishes to take as many as possible with him when he goes into eternal judgment.

Do not be deceived; the Scripture is clear. Christ did not fail in anything He came to do. If He said that we should believe in Him for salvation, then He has a plan as to how to work it out in us.

Is the change in one's life total and immediate? Or do we go from precept to precept, line upon line, line upon line, here a little, there a little? The Word speaks to both of these things, first of all in Isaiah 28:9–13 (KJV): "Whom shall he teach knowledge? and whom shall he make to understand doctrine? *Them that are* weaned from the milk, and drawn from the breasts. For precept *must be* upon precept, precept upon precept; line upon line, line upon line; here a little, *and* there a little: For with stammering lips and another tongue will he speak to his people. To whom he said, This *is* the rest *wherewith* ye may cause the weary to rest; and this *is* the refreshing; yet they would not hear. But the word of the Lord was unto them precept upon precept, precept upon precept; line upon line, line upon line; here a little, *and* there a little; that they might go, and fall backward, and be broken, and snared, and taken."

Here the Lord is instructing the people in the way they should go in order to show them they can't make it on their own. The Lord has laid out everything in a neat little package for them, but they don't get it in the end. Here the Scripture is speaking as to the pride of the people. Is this not what happened to me in the first chapter of this book when I did not heed God's instruction? Just like the ones He is speaking to in this passage of Isaiah.

The children of Ephraim had made a covenant with the world. And they were to receive of the world its judgment, unless they followed the precepts line upon line as the Lord had instructed them. The Lord says He gave them this instruction, knowing they would not keep it. What is the provision the Lord made for His people then? Isaiah 28:16: "Therefore thus saith the Lord God, Behold, I lay in Zion for a foundation a stone, a tried stone, a precious corner *stone,* a sure foundation: he that believeth shall not make haste."

Here the Lord is telling us to wait upon Him and not to put our trust in any other.

This is what I had to learn, that it was God's doing that delivered me from the act of my disobedience. It was God who delivered me from the results of the sin I agreed to. It was God that delivered me from the nightly spiritual raping I underwent for so many years. I believe that God will not deliver one who is not born again. There are those who believe not in Him—the previous Scriptures show this. I also believe that if we believe in the Lord and are saved, that the gift of life is within us and must find a way to give life outside of us, or perhaps we are not born again. Because this is the testimony of Christ Jesus in us, let us look to Romans 8:5: **"For they that are after the flesh do mind the things of the flesh;"** (This means they prefer to do these things in Galatians 5:19–21: "Now the works of the flesh are manifest, which are *these;* Adultery, fornication, uncleanness, lasciviousness, Idolatry, witchcraft, hatred, variance, emulations, wrath, strife, seditions, heresies, Envyings, murders, drunkenness, revellings, and such like: of the which I tell you before, as I have also told *you:* in time past, that they which do such things shall not inherit the kingdom of God.") **"But they that are after the Spirit**

the things of the Spirit." (Prefer to do the things in; Galatians 5:22–23: "But the fruit of the Spirit is love, joy, peace, longsuffering, gentleness, goodness, faith, Meekness, temperance: against such there is no law.")

Romans 8:13–14: "For if ye live after the flesh, ye shall die: but if ye through the Spirit do mortify the deeds of the body, ye shall live. For as many as are led by the Spirit of God, they are the sons of God."

Romans 8:24–30: "For we are saved by hope: but hope that is seen is not hope: for what a man seeth, why doth he yet hope for? But if we hope for what we see not, *then* do we with patience wait for it. Likewise the Spirit also helpeth our infirmities: for we know not what we should pray for as we ought: but the Spirit itself maketh intercession for us with groanings which cannot be uttered. And he that searcheth the heart knoweth what is the mind of the Spirit, because he maketh intercession for the saints according to the *will of* God. And we know that all things work together for good to them that love God, to them who are called according to *his* purpose. For whom he did foreknow, he also did predestinate *to be* conformed to the image of his Son, that he might be the firstborn among many brethren. Moreover whom he did predestinate, them he also called: and whom he called, them he also justified: and whom he justified, them he also glorified."

In my life, I have never seen someone who could do what Christ Jesus has done for us. History does not record anyone putting themselves to the trials which are another's as did Jesus. What a price to pay!; There are some who believe that a saved person can lose his or her salvation, but in this portion of Scripture, we see to what lengths the Lord went to, to secure those who believe in Him.

I believe that salvation is both immediate and a process. I read in the above Scriptures that those who are called by God, and those who hope for salvation, are those who seek God. I believe also that we will learn line upon line and precept upon precept. And this is not in any way the indication of salvation.

This passage of Scripture clearly indicates that man does not know what to pray for in relation to his salvation. This Scripture speaks of those who *love* God and follow after Him.

I believe that there are those who have tried to follow Jesus but have not asked His help in doing so. I believe the Scripture is clear they do not have salvation. It is clear that one must be willing to respond to all that is ask of oneself in order to receive salvation. Here! This indicates a response from us to the leading of the Holy Spirit to acknowledge who Christ Jesus is and to believe in Him and His testimony. That is the gospel of Jesus Christ.

Predestination is not some kind of super trick that God plays to determine who will enter; The Kingdom of Heaven. The word means He knows the beginning from the end and is faithful to bring those who love him into the Kingdom of God at the appointed time. This is the case where everyone was invited but not everyone's choice is to come. The example is the time of Noah when people were so much into themselves that they never gave God the time of day and were not interested in what Noah was doing except to ridicule him.

I think today many people feel that someone else should be responsible for their lack of interest. I think these people are so involved with themselves and self-gratification that it would seem they want to be held without recompense;

that their free ride never stops. They count on the goodness of other people to enable their directionless trekking across the pages of life.

What did God tell me when I enquired of Him to go with me and straighten out what was going on in the hedge across the street? God said, "I wouldn't go if I were you." As I have testified to you, my ideas were not profitable at all.

Is it because I had a unique experience and it couldn't happen to any other person? The Scripture in Ecclesiastes 9:2 says, "All *things come* alike to all: *there is* one event to the righteous, and to the wicked; to the good and to the clean, and to the unclean; to him that sacrificeth, and to him that sacrificeth not; as *is* the good so *is* the sinner; *and* he that sweareth, as *he* that feareth an oath."

It seems to me that all have the same opportunity in life to follow the leading of God's direction. When one chooses to go another direction, then one is one's own protector, discerner, guide, and judge. My question is still the same one: Can a five-year-old operate on a knowledge base which has no outside instruction?

The road map of life is God's design that whosoever forsakes it will be directionless. Good luck to all!

Chapter Eight

Has Happened to Others Too

As has happened to others, my life had other events which I experienced. As a person who is learning to get back on the right track, I have areas of my life still to deal with.

There are things which one has done that bring about circumstances to other lives. There are three such events in my life that did just that. When I got the message from Uncle Sam to be part of his military, the restraints I had managed to keep hold on for most of my life left me. When the opportunity came, I gave in to all the impulsive behavior every other young person has to deal with. I know most young people at that time of life must have had better luck dealing with things than I did, or at least I hope they did.

For me, going into the service meant celebrating my entering independence as well as saying good-bye to my friends. Drinking and being available for whatever came was a bad mix. I managed to impregnate two girls the night before I had to report for induction into the Navy.

The first girl wasn't someone I had chosen to be with, but when going to a friend's house to see if he wanted to go drinking with me, I found his sister home alone. For some reason she wanted, like myself, to be an investigator. She was my friend's sister. And I did not want to stay. But trying to say no was not what she wanted to hear. When I tried to leave, she would yell, "He is trying to rape me!" And if I stayed, she would not yell. So, thinking that going to jail the night before being inducted was not such a good thing, I stayed.

She was curious as to the plumbing parts, an area which had given me trouble all my life. I gave it a go at talking her out this. But each time I tried to leave, she would yell, "He's trying to rape me!" So I gave it one last attempt at stopping the investigation. I told her she would have to go all the way or no show-and-tell. I thought this would scare her out of any further investigation. It didn't work. We did, and that was the first of the two acts of irresponsibility on my part that evening.

The second act of irresponsibility was with someone who I had had a crush on in high school. But I had no guts in trying to get acquainted with her. After my interlude with the first girl—I am not trying to make my irresponsible act seem less important than it was, but I'm just trying to continue with my acts of infamy—I headed for Main Street and found one of the guys that I hung out with. And he joined me in my drinking. As we cruised around town that night, I happened to run across the girl I had had a crush on in high school. She was with another girl and I asked if they wanted to cruise around town for a while. The two girls came over to the car and wanted to talk.

The girl I had the crush on said she might want to cruise around with me, if I would walk on Main Street with her so everyone could see us together. That would take an hour or so.

Well, I thought I had died and gone to heaven! This girl wanted to be seen with me. Little did I know how much she wanted to see of me! As we walked around town, she told me that she wasn't interested in getting married. Because all men; in her estimation were not to be trusted. She wanted to have a child but not to be married. This was kind of a new thought to me because I had always imagined what it would be like to marry her. And now to find out she didn't want that kind of relationship. This was a bummer to say the least. But after having been already with someone that night, I figured I wasn't going to be any worse for what she suggested than what had already taken place. So we did.

The third act of irresponsibility took place around a year later in Japan. My ship was in dry dock for some upgrades. Liberty passes were a frequent accessibility for those who did their work on time. So being one who most always got my work done, I had liberty quite often. Liberty was restricted to areas approved by the captain of the ship. Well, of course that meant do not get caught out of bounds. Right!

Well, on one of those out-of-bounds trips, I found a bar that had a lot of girls who sported themselves—they were hookers. With a lot of liquor, one does not need too much persuasion and I managed to impregnate another girl. I did not find this out until some years later. This girl (woman) had come to the United States to work for a company that I hauled product to in my truck-driving job.

The first woman to have my child was but fourteen years old. After she was grown up, I found out that she had had my child.

The second woman wrote me while in the navy. And she asked at the insistence of her parents if I wanted to marry her and take responsibility for her. In our conversation before I got her pregnant, she expressed that it would do no good to try to be the father. It was her desire not to be married. I declined the responsibility. (Yes, I was a real heal, self-centered, and the scum of life.)

The third woman, the one from Japan, came to the States to work and also asked me about our son. I knew this to be true because one night, when the ship I was on started to the Mediterranean, I got real sick so sick I prayed and asked God what had happened. And He said the woman in Japan was going to have a miscarriage. But if I wanted her to have the child, then He would see her through and the child would be born. I said yes.

These women all deserved a better life than they had received. I wasn't a help to any of them. I will not try to make an excuse so as to make myself the victim by trying to blame these women for all that took place. There is no taking back the actions one does to another person's life. Time flows only one way. And prevents anyone from going back and undoing any wrong's we commit. There is only going forward. To say I'm sorry for being the person I was doesn't change what has happened. However if anyone is to live in the way God intended men to live, change must take place. That is why responding to the leading of God's Holy Spirit is so critical in a person's life.

As I mentioned earlier in this book, living a life based on five-year-olds experiences and not having the presence of God to sustain your life is a life which cannot process all of the challenges. This confronts one's passage through this life. A person's days are short and each step is marked by what we do. Calling on the Creator of all life is the only option to bringing about healing and redirection for one's life, being the victim or perpetrator. As we cannot go back, we must heal.

It is an assumption that people are inherently endowed with all the skills that are necessary to live a successful life. This however just happens to be the wrong assumption.

But nevertheless, if we take an honest assessment of history, what is required is to be tutored by a parent's life experiences or the experiences of another adult person or persons. We require directions from outside sources in order to assess what our need is. We are not all-knowing beings. This brings a question: was our parent's all-knowing or was their trek through life without the influences of others? I think not.

What I would like to relate is not self-justification for one's life, which is somehow a way to blame others for what I lacked in character, but that we all need to have direction, which is not just how I get what I need. But how do I relate good, sound, responsible actions among others? Where does our healing come from?

Chapter Nine

THINGS IN LIFE

One's life is filled with many things, and in 1978 I married my first wife. She was a dainty little woman with a semi-truck load of hurt and destruction in her life. Being a Christian, I should have married her for all the right reasons. Those would be need, the kind of need which is full of righteous passion, expressing thankfulness to God's provision for a life that complements God's desired intimacy with man.

The world has described love between men and women in every conceivable fashion with words which paint, in part, the estimation of beauty, desire, compulsions, and commitments as to the length of one's imagination. All the while they know they're lucky to have someone who wants to trek across life with them. Some marriages are blessed and some are not. The motive for marriage probably plays a large part in the outcome.

Such was the case of my first marriage. We often think that one day the natural occurrences of man will find their way in the rustle of life's experiences and *Wow! Here it is! Take it and go with it.*

I had a pastor who was himself unfaithful to his own life. And no matter who came into my life, he would put me down to them. At this point one could say God may not have wanted me to marry any of these women who I came to know. I agree it may not have been the best for them or them for me. God says even the rocks are able to cry out, so why not a wayward pastor?

Now to state right off, my motives for marrying my first wife were not righteous. She simply was someone I meet and she had no connection with my church or anyone in it. She had great need and so did I. But neither of us was caring about the needs of the other—only our own needs.

We were both running from oppression. This should have been grounds for a strong union. But a union can't stand when your concerns are more for yourself than the one you're with.

My main reason was if I got married, perhaps I would not be spiritually raped any longer. I also wanted to show those who opposed me having a relationship with someone that I didn't need them. And truly I didn't. But in guilt, a person tends to have little sense of responsibility or worth.

I tried to maintain as many ties as possible. I wanted my church at the time because I had seen my family all accept the Lord, and I wanted to rejoice with them as they gained freedom in the blessings of God.

Speaking like this sounds as if I was a total loss. God could not have been working in my life. I would most certainly have been in rebellion. Guess what? You're right! I was in rebellion.

Thankfully God is not me. He is faithful and, though he had to endure my tantrums and self-centered ways, the pride I displayed must have been the foulest of stench. God did not leave me, but with a righteous and loving hand of correction brought me and I hope my first wife through a time of turmoil and frustration as we tried to justify ourselves during the time when things were being terminated.

My first wife had two boys who were good kids. But they never should have had to go through what they did.

Looking back, if I had taken the time to wait and see where God wanted me to be in relation to my first wife, perhaps I would not have brought her pain as a result of my actions in marrying her.

Isaiah 40:31 says, "But they that wait upon the Lord shall renew *their* strength: they shall mount upon wings as eagles; they shall run, and not be weary; *and* they shall walk, and not faint." 1 Timothy 5:8 says, "But if any provide not for his own, and especially for those of his own house, he hath denied the faith, and is worse than an infidel." I not only was not looking out for myself, I didn't believe in the promises of God. The state I was in was a state of frustration and impatience. Instead of relying on God's strength and provision, I trusted myself once again.

If only I had waited, I could say I waited upon the Lord and He renewed my strength I now mount on wings as eagles. And I walk and do not faint. Perhaps one day I will be able to declare that boldly and with thanksgiving when I meet God face to face. For now I fall short.

I would have either not married or I would have been attentive to her needs. And the outcome would not have been as it was.

In the course of life, marriage and other relationships are of great importance. Where we walk with God and are led of the Spirit, we are able to look through the eyes of our Savior and Redeemer with love and compassion.

Unfortunately the relationship of the world to the church has brought compromise. People today are desensitized to God's plan for the regard of marriage and trust and relationships with others.

How can this be? Doesn't God protect those who believe in Him? Much of Scripture says this. Why are we so vulnerable? Why can't I overcome some of these things I have? They just seem to hang on and on. It's a question asked by all men.

One answer can be that the world has taught us what humility is. According to what the world's standard of humility is, this humility is in actuality pride. It says, "See what I have done for these. Now you must do likewise or you care nothing and your words are empty." The focus is on performance and not on righteousness, and the church has bought it hook, line, and sinker. So look at what we've done.

Someone is sure to say, "Is this not what the Bible says? Are we not supposed to help others?" But the world also says, "If I but help even one person, it is worth it?" (Of course helping *a* person is worth it.) But the world is setting the stage for the measure of help needed to be given. Saying most are not worthy to be helped, are these not the words of those who prepare to justify the very act before it occurs? It is an act of justification. They seek not to help people but rather, as happened with me, making a show of my commitment and not my love.

In chapter 1 of this book, I related what the Lord spoke to me. And I disobeyed His instruction, which resulted in years of not being able to access God's direction. And I was left to try to understand life based upon a five-year-old's knowledge that presented the direction in my life. It was the tree of knowledge of good and evil. I had opened the door to the presentations of principalities and powers and wickedness in high places. It wasn't my knowledge base which was in charge, it was the performance of what I viewed that began to form my way. That instructed my thoughts and formed the building blocks in my life.

I spoke of my fight to overcome the sexual attacks in my life and that I am thankful that the Lord had not let me through high school hurt anyone. That had to be the prayers of my mom or perhaps God was working on my behalf and I didn't know it.

1 John 3:18–24 says, "My little children, let us not love in word, neither in tongue; but indeed in and in truth. And hereby we know that we are of the truth, and shall assure our hearts before him. For if our heart condemns us, God is greater than our heart, and knoweth all things. Beloved, if our heart condemn us not, *then* we have confidence toward God. And whatsoever we ask, we receive of him, because we keep his commandments, and do those things that are pleasing in his sight. And this is his commandment, That we should believe on the name of his Son Jesus Christ, and love one another, as he gave us commandment. And he that keepeth his commandments dwelleth in him, and he in him. And hereby we know that he abideth in us, by his Spirit which he hath given us."

What am I saying in this chapter about my first marriage and relationships with others? Even when we know God, as a born-again child of God, God does not take us out of the world. God directs us through the canyons and hazards of this world. These are the events which challenge our walk with God. They are sometimes greater *than our trust* in God's ability to preserve our way. So what happens is we are given an opportunity to stand and observe the up-close workings of Satan first hand.

Does this mean that we turned away from God and are lost to burn in hell as some churched peoples tell us? I will in part, answer this question with a question. Who is it that saves? Is it God or is it us? If God is able to save us (God is able, says Ephesians 3:20: "Now unto him that is able to do exceeding abundantly above all that we ask or think, according to the power that worketh in us."), then we must be the saved, right?

1 John 3:20: "For, if our hearts condemn us, God is greater than our hearts, and knoweth all things."

1 John 4:10: "Herein is love, not that we loved God, but that he loved us, and sent his Son *to be* the propitiation for our sins."

John 3:3 says, "Jesus answered and said unto him, Verily, verily, I say unto thee, Except a man be born again, he cannot see the kingdom of God."

The Greek word for born is "gennao, *ghen-nah'-o*; from a variation of 1085; to *procreate* (properly of the father, but by extension of the mother); figuratively to regenerate:- bear, begat, be born, bring forth, conceive, be delivered of, gender, make, spring."

The above Scriptures: and the word born; point to only one Savior. That is the Lord Jesus. Jesus requires that we believe in what He has done for us. The Holy Spirit makes intersession in prayer for the things we do not know how to pray for. The father is the one that brings forth the saved person, as we see in John 3:3.

In America where I live, people have known freedom and also are easily seduced by the ways of the world. This brings unreal concepts of what has happened. And it applies to how we receive God's Word. One aspect of this is we are the ones responsible for everything that occurs in our life. Reason is we have arrogance that it is us who saves us. We say it is Jesus for those who are in the Christian faith, but as we make the confession we determine that it is really us who has the contract for salvation. And it's up to us. Jesus is just the initial focal point for what we have to do. My prayer is for God to help us.

My second marriage I thought was in a righteous context. I loved this woman and was committed to whatever it took to make it work. This lady had three boys whom I loved as well. I still do, even after the marriage failed. What went wrong? My body just wore out. I could not maintain a living to support the needs of family and also unfortunately the needs of my wife.

The little girl we adopted was like the spring in my heart. I miss her and the boys very much. As for my ex-wife, she remarried. I pray for God's blessing in her life. Here is where I called on the Lord for direction and believed everything was of the leading of God.

The one variable in both marriages was the working of principalities and powers in high places. These are things that we can overcome. But if we get too distracted, then the enemy can sneak in and take control of things in a way which will cause us to fight on to many fronts. This causes the battle to be sometimes lost. What do you do from here? I believe the Bible says, "Stand" when you have done all, *stand!*

Take up where you have ended up and seek God's direction. Get back on track. It is not you who save's, but God.

Chapter Ten

OVERWHELMED

There comes a time in everyone's life when so many things have presented themselves that to be able to orderly file each occurrence under the title of *handled successfully* is no longer possible. The fallen nature of man was no help from the start.

Here I am now in this chapter, the one which begins to illustrate the times of remorse. *The Wikipedia, the free encyclopedia* defines; remorse as the following: "Remorse is an emotional expression of personal regret felt by a person after he or she has committed an act which they deem to be shameful, hurtful, or violent."

Remorse, living with the consequences of having disobeyed God, is a feeling that, if acknowledged, can bring salvation and redemption.

When I crossed the fence at five years old and saw what was happening, I tried to be strong and be in control. But when God's presence is no longer the intimate direction of the heart and is replaced with direction from self or another, your secure world collapses. As one retains the memory of what used to be, one is converted into something different by that which now directs their lives: seduction.

Can you imagine trading a new car off for an old clunker? Doesn't make sense, does it? Why are we so willing to ditch God for a lost cause like Satan? And it isn't just five-year-olds who do it!

As I look back, I wonder what a relationship I might have had with God if I would have just listened and obeyed what He said. Maybe all those years would have been so blessed that I could have had a tremendously filled life, able to seek God at any time I needed help and He would have spoken the answer right then and there. But I'll never know because I chose a different path.

I think about how my life evolved and how much it was controlled by the choice I made at such a young age. The church must have been asleep in those days or else was so busy perfecting its approach to God. Why was the church having trouble sharing its faith? Perhaps it too, like me, had decided to listen to another voice.

I know that I'm not the only one the Devil ever convinced to turn away from God. I hope that the others were able to find restoration with God a lot sooner than I did.

Knowing what is happening, and you can't do anything about it until you are reconnecting with God, is painful because you set the rules by which you are entering the rest of your life. Repenting of those rules is not easy and requires commitment. You soon find out that being in the grace of God is not a study in science but in humility. It isn't something you do but something you receive.

2 Corinthians 10:12: "For we dare not make ourselves of the number, or compare ourselves with some that

commend themselves: but they measuring themselves by themselves, and comparing themselves among themselves, are not wise."

Proverbs 22:15 (KJV): "Foolishness is bound in the heart of a child; but the rod of correction shall drive it far from him."

Paul is reminding us when we are under our own direction, or under someone other than God, that we are going to have conflict with God. Proverbs shows that there are things which need to be dealt with.

Knowledge; the Bible says we perish for lack of knowledge. Satan says the same thing. Remember Eve in the garden of Eden and how the serpent convinced Eve that knowledge was to be valued above obedience. I really believe that Satan starts working on us the moment we pop out of the womb of our mothers. There seem to be different gifts in people which they have from the moment they are conceived. For me, it was to know about everything: the what, when, why, and where. This is a sure fit as a mark for Satan's style of influence. I guess you could say I was *prime rib* for the cooking. I already had the ingredients for searching out things. And it is obvious Satan didn't need to pressure me hard to look into things.

While breath is still available, there is an open door for repentance. Getting a new life is not hard if you're willing to lay down the old one.

Asking Jesus into your life is asking to be saved and much more. It is asking for a new life connected to assurance in hope. This new life comes with a personal coach and confidant. The direction of your new life is provided through a trusted trainer, The Holy Spirit. Your life is overseen by God the Father. And Jesus is ministering at the right hand of the throne of God for your success. Remember He lost only one that the Father gave Him, and that was the son of perdition.

If you are like me, you will remember most everything. But if we leave it in God's hands and let the Holy Spirit do His work in us, then we will not have to endure the condemnation of God's judgment.

Romans 8:1: "There is therefore now no condemnation to them which are in Christ Jesus, who walk not after the flesh, but after the Spirit."

Chapter Eleven

BLESSINGS TO BE HAD

As there are new blessings to be had for each new day, there are also issues. When looking back at my life and seeing what I encountered through the years, I'm able to understand some of the hardships that others are going through.

We fight against principalities and powers, which are not readily visible to the eye. This brings a questioning as to whether or not it is I who is going wrong. Or am I getting some bad information that is steering my ability to make good judgments?

Ultimately if we follow bad choices we will have greater and greater trouble in our lives. According to Genesis 1:26, "And God said, let us make man in our image, after our likeness: and let him have dominion over the fish of the sea, and the over the foul of the air, and over the cattle, and over all the earth, and every creeping thing that creepeth upon the earth."

Now being made in the likeness of God, we have many good attributes. Being able to understand things is one, so we are able to receive instruction and make judgments as to the fit of *it* in all that we do. We have the ability to weigh the information and to compile that information, and compare the fit of that information with what we have already compiled and by assessment make a decision. All that said, it means we are able to learn. Other gifts of God are emotion, joy, hope, perception, peace, comfort, confidence, purpose, and authority.

There's a saying in relation to one's physical health: "You put junk in, you get junk out." In other words, our lives are *only* patterned after this kind of concept. We are consumers of all that God provides. And if there would not have been a tree of knowledge of good and evil in the garden of Eden., then we would be consuming only good.

However there was a tree of knowledge of good and evil. Plus the manager of the evil was present to sell his wares. He did so with great insight into seduction, which motivates the emotions, bringing stimulation which is often discerned as pleasure. When this takes place, it is hard to determine the motive that is working to persuade the learning potential of the participants.

In other words, there is good and evil and there is God and (Satan, the fomenter of evil). We are all sponges that must choose what we drink into our lives.

Have you ever watched Judge Judy on TV? If so, you've seen the presentations. How, in that mess of information, is a single person supposed to make the right call? Now I'm not judging Judge Judy as to her beliefs or habits but rather trying to show an extreme.

If Judge Judy is a Christian, she probably is on her knees a lot just to keep her sanity; if not, maybe she drinks a lot. But for sure she has had to find a way to cope with so much information. One way is to be informed on what is expected of the subject dealt with. That is what this life is all about: to know how to live it!

God's guidance and love give us the assurance that what we decide is in accordance with His plans. If we do not make God the focus in our lives, then there is another, which like a fungus will consume us.

This has been my testimony. This is the way God has molded my life. Is God finished with me yet? No! But like all who believe in and put their trust in Him, I know He will not fail to bring me all the way. And my testimony is not over, nor the praise will I give my Lord for His love. I am Greg Booth and tomorrow's a new day in which to be blessed.

Afterword

What I want to leave you with is this: the Lord God, since He created heaven and earth, has not failed to make a way for mankind to have a way of escape. Escape from what? Escape death; as the result of man's sin.

Let me use the metaphor of the computer after it was created. Now it is plain to the simplest mind of man that the early computers couldn't match the imagination of man's mind.

The opposite is true of God's fashioning of man. Man's ability, if not checked by God's loving grace, could have done most anything. Today's fast-paced development of technologies and their related by-products are advancing rapidly.

Computers are like man in many ways. Both were created, both functioned well at first, and then there was interference that presented a disease into the functioning process. For man, the original sin was introduced by Satan through beguiling Eva and Adam in the garden of Eden; the computer got its sentence when it received a virus ministered by a satanic type of program. Well, the results are both man and computer crashed. Both man and computer failed and were in need of a repairman. A real *geek*, meaning they both needed someone qualified to repair their fallen state.

The computer would be taken to a technician. The man would be tended by God who made him. Real problems need real answers.

I've said all this to let you know there is an enemy for everyone and everything that exists. The destroyer will never quit doing what works for him.

As long as there's time and existence as we know it, the enemy will be looking to hurt us anytime, anyway, anywhere he can. It is his nature to do so. Therefore if we are not watching, we can be drawn into the abyss of unconcern, oblivious to what is happening around us. How does the pickpocket manage to lift your wallet without you knowing it? Perhaps by getting you to focus on something else?

Acts that draw our attention keep us from maintaining focus on where we are at. This is sort of like when I got progressive trifocal glasses. I tried to walk over logs and rocks when I went hunting, but if I hunted like I normally had, I would have had to focus not on my feet but where I was looking, for the glasses presented a new aspect to my field of vision.

Having to adjust to how we view the circumstances taking place in our lives and the mechanisms through which we are engaged, when not in a normal routine or pattern of learned behavior causes us to focus on one thing longer than another. This would be the time in which we need to learn to adjust.

I confess I stumbled over rocks and logs as well as my own feet for some time in adjusting to my glasses while hunting in unfamiliar country. This is a pickpocket's ideal approach to finding someone who is out of their element. This is when their focus is most easily captured. This is when we become the target or the hunted.

This was in real time for me in my life as this book indicates. Even when in the presence of God's voice and His instruction, the enemy of my soul drew my focus away from the importance of what the Lord was speaking to me. In the book, I mentioned Ecclesiastes 9:2 about how all things come alike to all. Well, writing this book of my experiences in life isn't meant as a way to pander your self-gratification in life by trying to show you that, because it happened to someone else, it should be okay in my life.

The acts which our lives are involved in are a result of our choices, be they for good or evil. But when we think we are so much in control and are not able to be overcome in our lives by anything this world has to offer, and then; we are most vulnerable to attack. Why? When we are so focused on our own desires, we are not observing the approach of the predator stalking us.

How should we conduct our lives? Good question. My answer is this: Live for now and eternity.

What do I mean?

To live, it is required to stay alive. That means we need to observe to accomplish certain functions daily. We require the following:

Food.

Drink.

Sleep, or at minimum rest.

To be able to obtain food and drink.

To have a basic knowledge of our surroundings to know where the things we need exist and what it will take to acquire them.

To observe the boundaries that protects others and us.

This is where the awareness of our surroundings has influence on our lives.

This is also where we learn the survival skills needed for our lives.

To begin to know the limits of our territory so as to protect our availability to these basic needs.

The above list speaks about our responsibility and that to just take care of us requires a lot of effort on our part. This shows the basics for living now in the flesh. *But what about eternity?* How do we go through this physical life to a life of eternity? The answer is quite simple: just to die in the flesh will bring us into eternity. It's as simple as falling off a log.

Well, it would seem as if there's nothing to worry about because anyone can have eternal life. You're right—anyone can and everyone will. But just as is required for the physical life in the now, one should prepare to live the spiritual life of eternity.

In most every way, the physical mirrors the eternal. As we are passing through the physical, we are forced to look at boundaries and choices which will govern how we are to survive the time of physical presence in life.

When observing life in the physical, we will perceive the governance of the spiritual and the difference of these to existences, the spiritual or the direction which is asserted in the physical. This is what forms the functioning of the character and operation of the physical existence of life.

The now or physical life expresses boundaries every day. So must the spiritual life express boundaries? The training grounds for fashioning the spirit; is done in the flesh by God through the Holy Spirit. Just like the baby in the womb of a mother, the spiritual life which God imparts to mankind needs time after conception to develop. Even when the Spirit of God is given in fullness, those sons of God need to be trained to function in the Spirit before entering into eternity. That length of time is determined by God alone.

I share in this book that we war against principalities and powers and not flesh and blood. However we are so enamored by the flesh that we tend to think that is all there is to life.

Why would this be so? We are told it is so over and over again. Satan, or the serpent in the garden of Eden, convinced Eva it was so. His suggestion was it would make her better than she thought she was. Taking the forbidden fruit made her reward death, both physically overtime and spiritually in separation from God.

As is rust to iron, a termite to wood, locust to a crop, and the swarming of ants to all that live—plants or flesh—so is the spirit of Satan to all mankind. Pride, power, lies, murder, lust, self-gratification, and any other detestable thing are the tools of Satan. Oh, yes, he is an expert! He is the best bad guy ever.

The seduction of Satan's way is subtle, not easily seen but, like an asp, very deadly to men in the flesh. This also will be eternal separation to God in eternity if they die without receiving salvation through gospel of Jesus Christ. Satan's way has toppled governments and slaughtered millions upon millions of people. Yet what do we see with the eye just a bunch of people; who can't get along? Just let them take care of their own problems.

What a buried-head-in-the-sand idea this is. We're so distracted watching evil being played out in others' lives that we're not aware that the creeping mist of God's judgment is on its way to meet us. After all, we are not concerned, for our own pride is telling us we are not touchable.

My aunt once had a plaque in her laundry room. On it was a man in a toilet with his hand on the flush handle. Above the picture, the caption said, "Good bye, cruel world." Please never become like this.

Many of us have had horrific experiences in life. However or whatever kinds these were, God has made a way to rescue you from your death. The Father God sent His most beloved to be your savior. His name is Jesus and His Spirit not only lives in those who believe on Him, but His flesh is at the right-hand throne of God making intersession for all who will believe in the gospel of Christ. Please be one of these who do believe. Then when you have received Jesus into life, trust Him for the remainder of your life in the flesh. The reward will be different from Eve's; yours will be the eternal presence of God.

The Bible says it is appointed once for every man to die. Christ is coming soon for the second time. If you die to self, then maybe you will not have to die physically because there will be some believers who are alive when Christ returns.

Now hear this, oh church. Put away your doctrines of men and obey the whole word of God. Leave nothing out which God has spoken. Though there may be in ratio like that which the Lord told Elijah in 1 Kings 19:18, there may be many who have not been taken in by the doctrines of men.

There is no excuse for the persecutions of the church, but the church itself. God's Word says we are the head and Satan is the tail. His head is to be crushed under the heel of the church. Church, there is no excuse for the way things have turned out. This crushing of Satan's influence is done in love by the great commission. We find this in Mark 16:15–18: "And he said unto them, Go ye into all the world, and preach the gospel to every creature. He that believeth and is baptized shall be saved; but he that believeth not shall be damned. And these signs shall follow them that believe; In my name they shall cast out devils; they shall speak with new tongues; they shall take up serpents; and if they drink any deadly thing, it shall not hurt them; they shall lay hands on the sick, and they shall recover."

Repent and honor God as He directs. It is never too late unless the return of Jesus finds the church wanting. Acts 17:30 "And the times of this ignorance God winked at; but now commandeth all men everywhere to repent:"

God made beauty and right from the start Satan found ways to throw dirt on it. How was he able to do this? By talking us into giving him access.

Vocabulary Notes

Words have great influence on our understanding of any text. Here are some examples of where the words used came from. We can see that these words where derived from a specific source. The word believe came from the Greek in this instance. The word till came from the Hebrew, and the word work; came from the American Century Dictionary.

The word: *believe*, and its assignment as to its meaning is of great importance. The way we view a particular word determines the depth of understanding of that word and its place of importance as to the depth of meaning of the Scripture passage it is used in.

The definition of the word: *believe;* as it is used in 1 John 3:23. It is up to you to determine the message of the Scripture which God is giving you.

The information about the word believe: is found below. I hope it will be of assistance in your search for the understanding of the direction God is taking your studies.

The word *till* in the Old Testament is also of great importance in understanding where man's place and authority have been assigned.

I suggest a challenge. Try to find Scriptures that have the meanings for the words that define *believe, till,* and *work*. Then figure out how they apply in your life today.

The information for Strong's was found on the Blue Letter Bible website.

http://www.blueletterbible.org/lang/lexicon/lexicon.cfm?Strongs=G4100&t=KJV*Believe,* as to its importance in knowing *salvation*. The meaning from Greek comes from *Strong's Concordance* 4100, which comes from 4102.

The word *believe* in Greek is *pisteuo* ("pist-yoo-o"), which means: as copied from the Blue Letter website.

"to think to be true, to be persuaded of, to credit, place confidence in

a. of the thing believed
to credit, have confidence

b. in a moral or religious reference
used in the NT of the conviction and trust to which a man is impelled by a certain inner and higher prerogative and law of soul
to trust in Jesus or God as able to aid either in obtaining or in doing something: saving faith
mere acknowledgment of some fact or event: intellectual faith to entrust a thing to one, i.e. his fidelity

c. to be intrusted with a thing"

The information for Strong's was found on the Blue Letter Bible website

http://www.blueletterbible.org/lang/lexicon/Lexicon.cfm?Strongs=G4102&t=KJV

Meaning from 4102, which come from 3982. The Greek word is *pistis* ("pis'-tis"), which means: as copied from the Blue Letter website

"conviction of the truth of anything, belief; in the NT of a conviction or belief respecting man's relationship to God and divine things, generally with the included idea of trust and holy fervour born of faith and joined with it

    a. relating to God
the conviction that God exists and is the creator and ruler of all things, the provider and bestower of eternal salvation through Christ

    b. relating to Christ
a strong and welcome conviction or belief that Jesus is the Messiah, through whom we obtain eternal salvation in the kingdom of God

    c. the religious beliefs of Christians

    d. belief with the predominate idea of trust (or confidence) whether in God or in Christ, springing from faith in the same fidelity, faithfulness

    e. the character of one who can be relied on"

The information for Strong's was found on the Blue Letter Bible website

http://www.blueletterbible.org/lang/lexicon/Lexicon.cfm?Strongs=G3982&t=KJV

Meaning from 3982. The Greek word is *peitho* ("pi'-tho"), which means: as copied from the Blue Letter website "persuade

    a. to persuade, i.e. to induce one by words to believe

    b. to make friends of, to win one's favour, gain one's good will, or to seek to win one, strive to please one

    c. to tranquillise

    d. to persuade unto i.e. move or induce one to persuasion to do something

be persuaded

    a. to be persuaded, to suffer one's self to be persuaded; to be induced to believe: to have faith: in a thing
to believe
to be persuaded of a thing concerning a person

    b. to listen to, obey, yield to, comply with

    c. to trust, have confidence, be confident"

Peitho is the Greek word that describes the outcome of the action involved with discovery and brings about inward certainty, which is supported through the evidence and assurances that are able to convince. Thereby it is accepted by the enquirer through conviction.

Pistis is the Greek word that speaks to having already been convinced of a specific matter; in the matter of moral conviction; concerning the religious truth of God; and concerning the reference as to Christ for salvation.

Pisteuo is the Greek word that means the trust and persuasion in; the reliance and constancy of profession. In conviction of moral trust, this is the credence in the religious acceptance of the gospel of Christ.

The information for Strong's was found on the Blue Letter Bible website.

http://www.blueletterbible.org/lang/lexicon/lexicon.cfm?Strongs=H5647&t=KJV**The word *till*,** from *Strong's Concordance.* Reference number is 5647. As copied from the Blue Letter website

"to work, serve

a. (Qal)
    to labour, work, do work
    to work for another, serve another by labour
    to serve as subjects
    to serve (God)
    to serve (with Levitical service)

b. (Niphal)
    to be worked, be tilled (of land)
    to make oneself a servant

    c.   (Pual) to be worked

    d.   (Hiphil)
to compel to labour or work, cause to labour, cause to serve
to cause to serve as subjects

    e.   (Hophal) to be led or enticed to serve"

The word work, as defined in *The American Century Dictionary* (first published in 1966).

Work is a noun meaning:

"application of mental or physical effort to a purpose; use of energy

task to be undertaken

thing done or made by work; result of an action

employment or occupation

literary or musical compositions

(pl.) operative part of a clock or machine

the works: colloquial:

    a.   all that is available or needed

    b.   full treatment

(pl.) operations of building or repair

(pl. often treated as singular) factory

(usually plural) meritorious act – adjective

of or used for work – verb

do work; be engaged in bodily or mental activity

be employed

craft (a material, etc.)

operate or function, especially effectively

operate; manage; control

    a. cause to toil

    b. manipulate

    c. cultivate (land)

    d. brings about; produce as a result

    e. colloquial, arrange (matters)

solve

bring to a desired shape or consistency

do or make needle work, etc.

make (one's way) gradually or with difficulty

gradually become (loose, etc.) by constant movement

artificially excite

    a. purchase with one's labor instead of money

    b. obtain by labor the money for

have influence

ferment

at work in action

work off, get rid of by work or activity

work out:

    a. solve or calculates

    b. solve; understand

    c. have a result

    d. provide for the details of

    e. engage in physical exercise or training

work over:

    a. examines thoroughly

    b. *slang*. beat up

work up:

    a. develop or advance gradually

    b. elaborate or excite by degree

    c. develop; devise [OE]"

www.ingramcontent.com/pod-product-compliance
Lightning Source LLC
LaVergne TN
LVHW020432080526
838202LV00055B/5148